Contents

The individual titles within this publication
are available as separate ebooks.

www.skillbuilderbooks.com

ISBN-13: 978-0-578-43947-1

A Note to Parents

Build skills one page at a time with Skill Builder ABC; 78 targeted activities that provide sensory enrichment and support foundational and functional motor skill development.

Each activity in the book is accompanied by a photograph showing how to perform the task, corresponding alphabet hand sign, and two sections of text. The main text is a rhyming couplet written in children's book style. It is a quick, fun, and engaging description of the activity. This gets kids interested and gives simple vocabulary to use when completing or discussing each task. The bottom text is designed to give teachers, parents, and caregivers more information about what the activity is addressing and its importance. This empowers adults with the knowledge of not only what to do to help kids develop skills, but how to do it, and why.

Whether you simply read through the book, do all the activities in a row, or something in between, know that each time a child interacts with Skill Builder ABC they are building skills for success.

Stacie Erfle, MS, OTR/L

Stacie Erfle, MS, OTR/L

www.skillbuilderbooks.com

Glossary

Fine Motor: Relating to the small muscles in the hands and fingers

Gross Motor: Relating to the large muscles in the arms, legs, and torso

Sensory: Relating to the eight senses

1. Auditory - hearing
2. Gustatory - taste
3. Interoceptive - internal sensations
4. Olfactory - smell
5. Proprioceptive - movement of the muscles and joints
6. Tactile - touch
7. Vestibular - movement and position of the head
8. Visual - sight

Fine Motor ABC

Alphabet Themed Activities to Strengthen Fine Motor Skills

Skill Builder Books

skillbuilderbooks.com

Stacie Erfle, MS, OTR/L

Aa

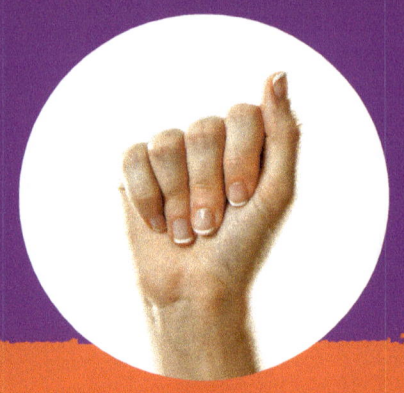

Move like an **animal** – bear crawl or crab walk.
Growl like a grizzly, but does a crab talk?

6

Upper extremity weight bearing prior to fine motor tasks provides input to the muscles and joints of the hands, arms, and shoulders. Called proprioceptive input, this facilitates body awareness and encourages coordinated movements.

Bb

Create a pattern when putting **beads** on a string. Make it repeat until you finish the whole thing.

The ability for the eyes and hands to work together effectively is called visual-motor integration or eye-hand coordination. It is foundational to all paper and pencil tasks, and is also required for activities such as stringing beads and catching a ball.

Cc

Curve your hand to make a **cup**.
Find some coins and fill it up.

Curving the hand develops the longitudinal arch. The arches of the hand make it possible to hold objects of various sizes and shapes.

Dd

Just like sewing, lace the string up and **down**.
Use any color – red, green, blue, or brown.

To support the development of hand dominance, a child should be encouraged to not switch hands during an activity. For example, if they start using their right hand to lace and their left hand to hold the lacing card, they should complete the task in that manner.

Ee

Left and right thumbs up, now cut on the line.
Sit up tall and keep your **elbows** close to your spine.

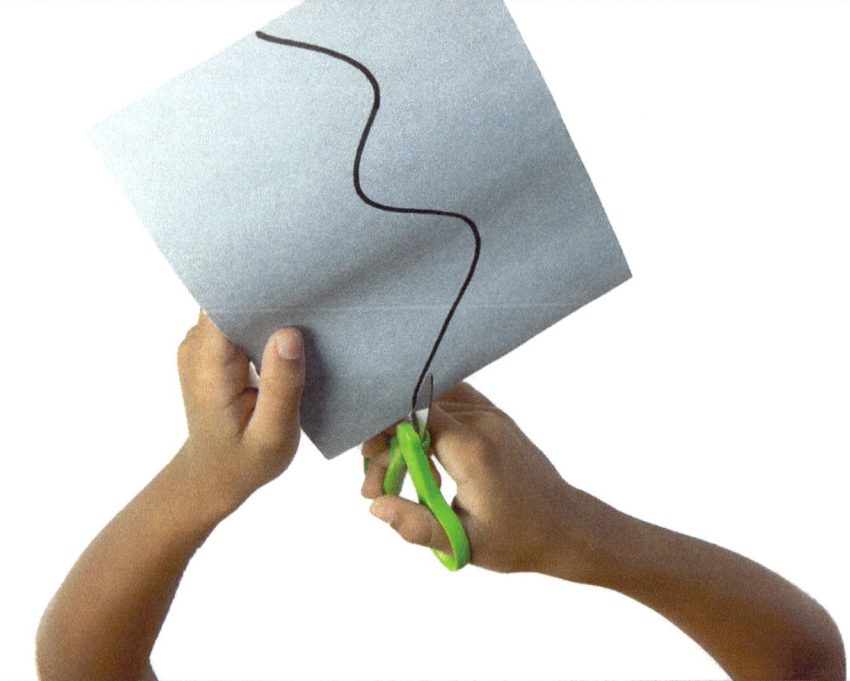

Effective positioning of the hands and body is required for successful performance of fine motor activities. Poor positioning makes a task more difficult and can impair a child's ability to develop age-appropriate skills.

Ff

Use your thumb and 2 fingers to make O's.
You can do it with your hands but not with your toes.

This position creates space between the thumb and index finger, called an open web space. It requires adequate strength and stability in the muscles of the thumb. When the web space is closed, the thumb is held against the side of the index finger, limiting a functional fingertip grasp.

Gg

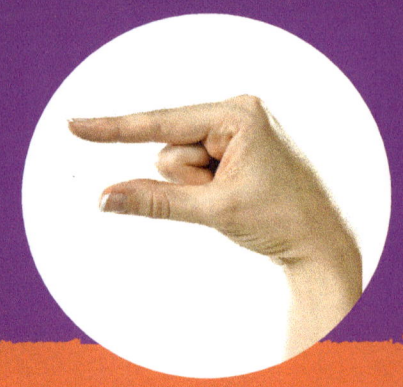

Peel the paper off broken crayons and then hold the tip. Using just your fingers will improve your **grip.**

A short crayon or pencil limits the opportunity for children to use atypical grasp patterns such as wrapping all fingers up the length of the writing tool.

Hh

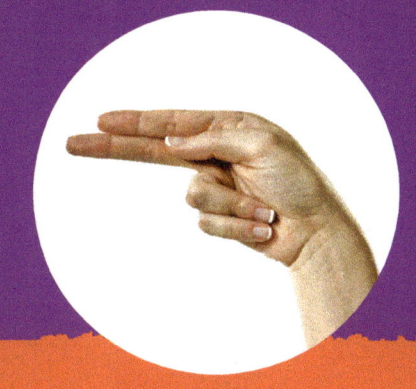

Draw a picture – you can kneel, sit, or stand.
Just don't forget to hold the paper with your **helping** hand.

13

Bilateral integration is the ability to coordinate the two sides of the body. One way this is done is by using the non-dominant helping hand to stabilize materials while the dominant working hand performs a task.

Ii

Make an 8 lying down, **imagine** it's fast asleep.
Trace over it 10 times without making a peep.

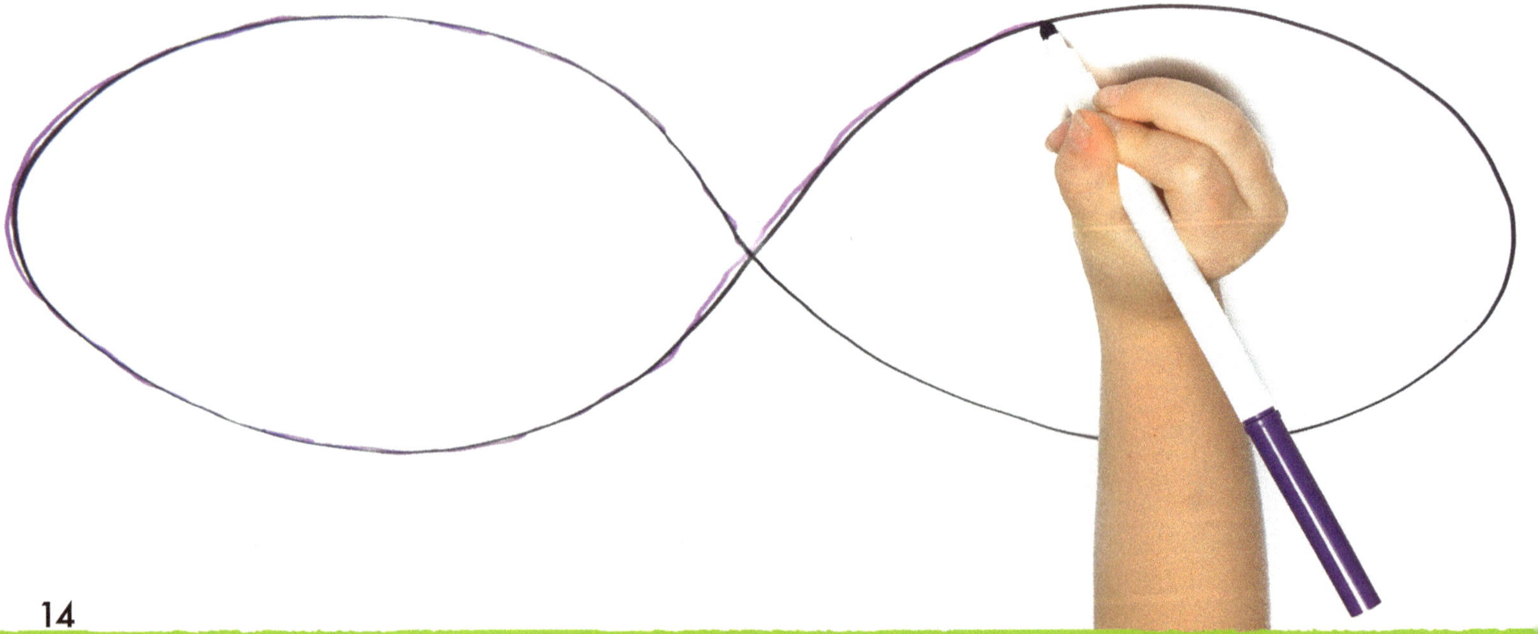

14

Crossing over the midline, or middle, of the body is required to develop hand dominance.
Having a highly skilled, dominant hand is needed for fine motor skills such as handwriting.
If a child writes with both hands, each hand will not have adequate practice opportunities
to become efficient.

Jj

Hold onto a treasure with 2 fingers tight.
Your other 3 fingers can hold the pencil **just** right.

The most common way to hold a pencil is a tripod grasp, using the thumb, index finger, and middle finger. Although this is ideal, there are many variations. The most important component is that the pencil grasp is functional and can produce writing with sufficient legibility and speed.

Kk

Move 5 pennies from fingertips to palm.
Try to keep them all in your hand, it's tricky, stay calm.

16

This kind of movement is referred to as translation. It is an example of in-hand manipulation, the ability to move objects using only one hand. These types of complex fine motor skills allow for effective object positioning.

Ll

Glue dried beans on the letters of your name.
Or do the whole alphabet and make it a game.

When picking up small items with the thumb and tip of the index finger, a child is using a pincer grasp. This grasp begins to develop in infancy and is needed for everything from self-feeding to holding a pencil.

Mm

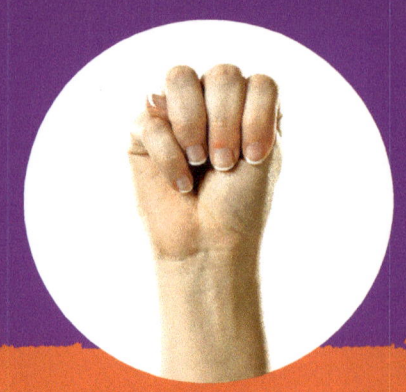

With tweezers or tongs **move** raisins around.
But please don't put them where they can't be found.

Grasp and release activities, such as tongs and spray bottles, develop the open and close motion required for using scissors.

Nn

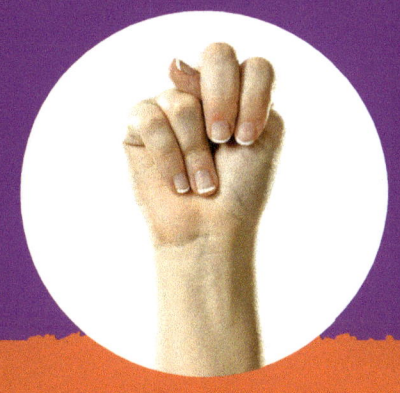

Build a paperclip chain link by link.
It could be a **necklace,** what do you think?

Not all fine motor activities need to be done at a table. A great alternative position that builds shoulder strength and stability is lying on the belly using the elbows to prop up the body. This position, called prone, can be used when drawing, doing puzzles, and manipulating small objects.

Tap your fingers **one** at a time.
Now you're playing the piano, just like a mime.

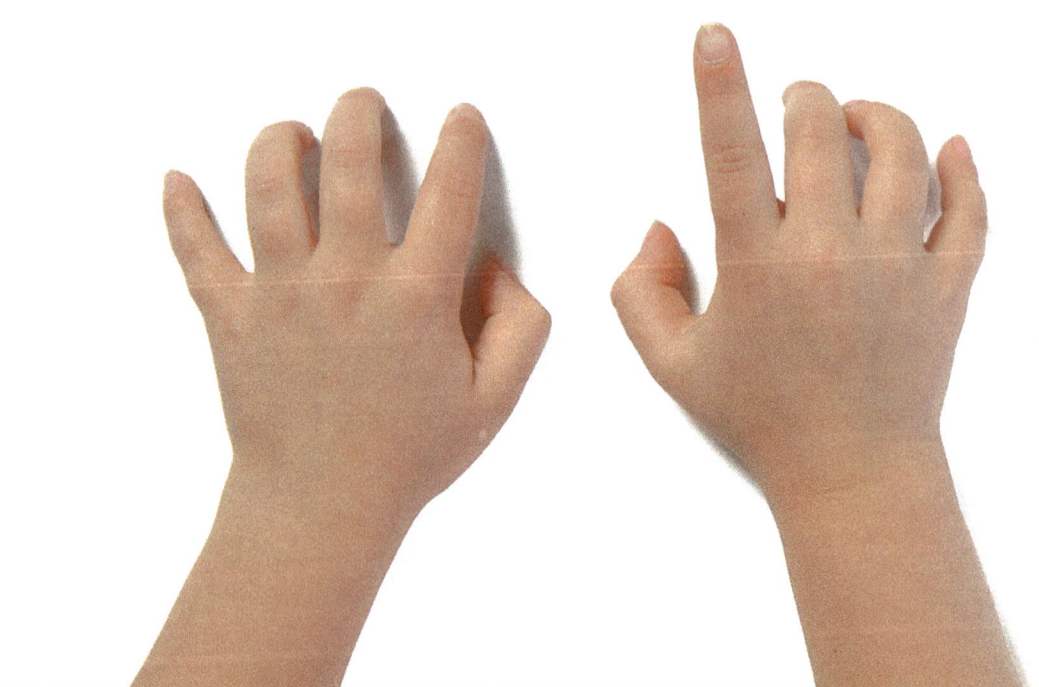

The ability to move fingers one at a time is called finger isolation. Fine motor skills require that the hand does not move as a unit, but that the fingers can work individually.

Pp

Use your thumb, **pointer,** and tall man to open a clothespin. Clip them to paper or the edge of a bin.

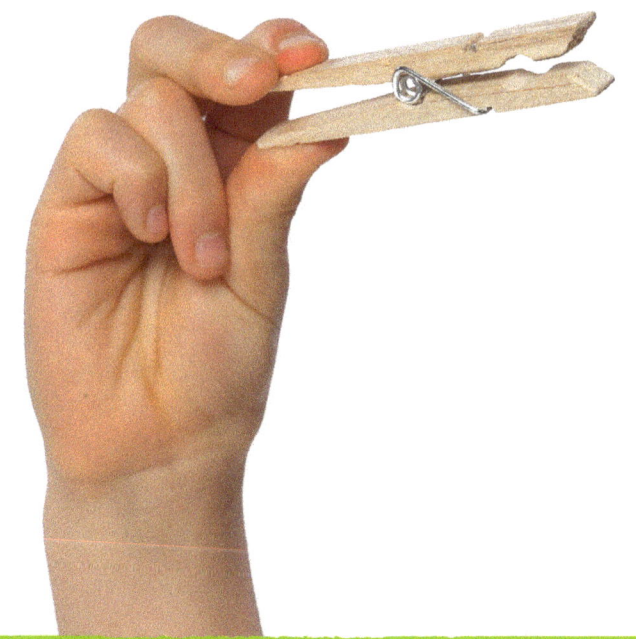

Tucking the ring and pinky fingers into the palm provides a stable base that allows the thumb, index finger, and middle finger to make precise movements. Known as hand separation, it is required for numerous fine motor skills including writing and cutting.

Qq

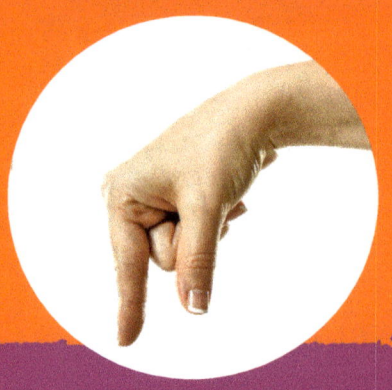

Turn into a plank, make your body a straight line.
Hold it for 10, don't quit, you're doing fine.

22

Postural control, the ability to maintain an upright body position, and shoulder strength are necessary for fine motor skills. A child with poor postural control will often tire easily when seated and will compensate by lying on or leaning against the table.

Rr

Roll out a long snake with some playdough.
Pinch from the head to the tail, left to right, and go slow.

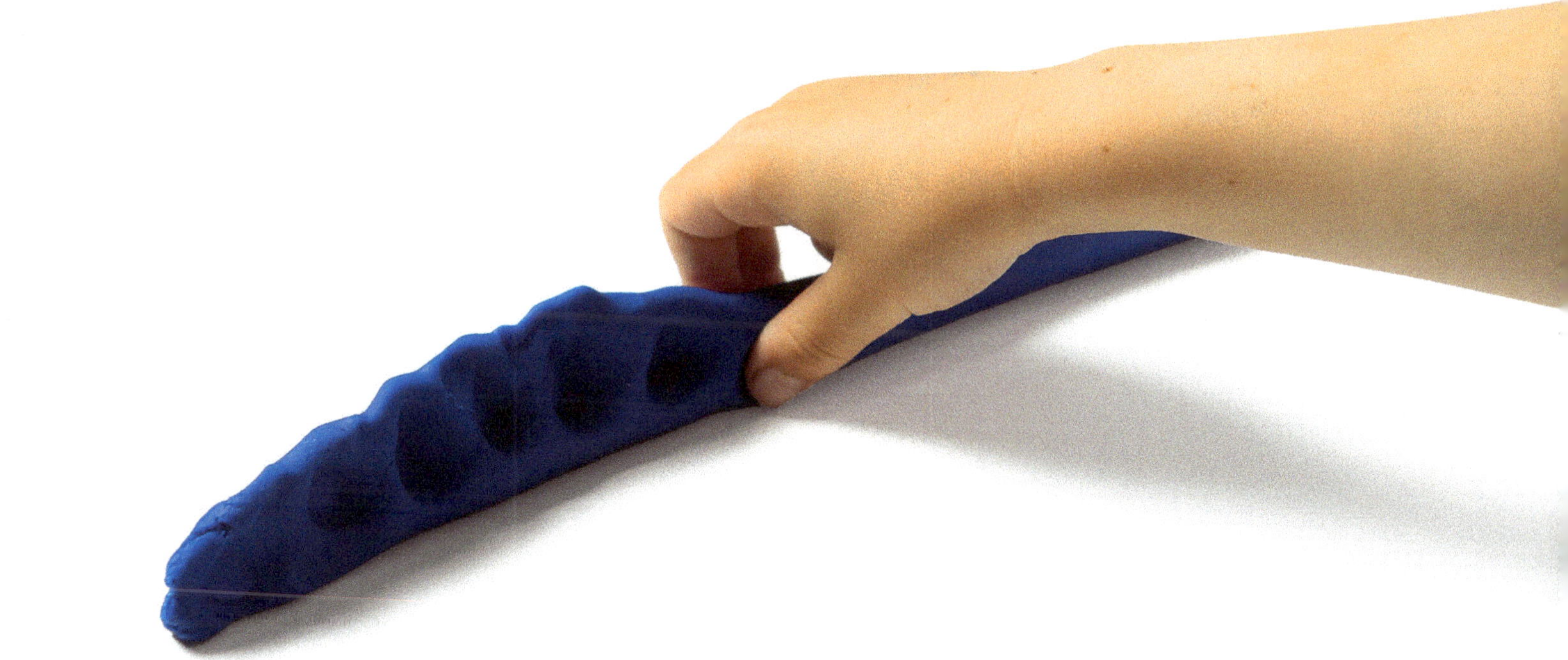

Pinching with the thumb, index finger, and middle finger strengthens the muscles needed for a tripod grasp. Playdough can also be squeezed, flattened, pounded, and squashed for hand strengthening.

Ss

Crumple paper with your fingertips into a ball.
Make 5 big and then make 5 small.

Strength and stability are both needed for efficient fine motor skills. Forming paper into a ball can strengthen the fingers; however, ensure that the thumb maintains a stable position and does not collapse at the base or pinch against the side of the index finger.

Tt

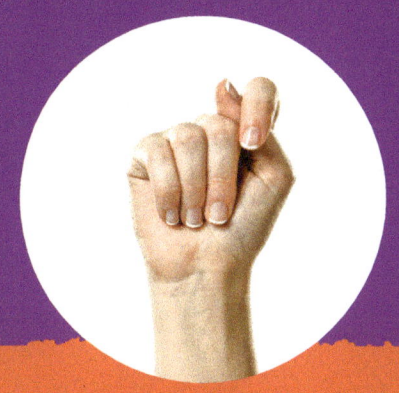

Find a cap and give it a twirl.
Pretend it's as precious as a clam with a pearl.

Rotating an object at the fingertips develops in-hand manipulation. Other examples include twirling a pencil and pushing a button through the hole. In-hand manipulation skills require thumb to finger opposition, the ability for the tip of the thumb to touch the tips of the fingers.

Uu

Color with your paper **up** on the wall.
Use plenty of tape so that it won't fall.

When working on a vertical surface, the wrist is naturally put into extension, with the back of the hand closer to the arm. This allows for improved thumb positioning and finger movements. Additionally, it inhibits wrist flexion, which is often used to compensate for poor wrist stability.

Vv

Use a **variety** of shapes to draw a person and frog. Then add the setting, some grass and a log.

Drawing pictures not only supports literacy development, but builds a foundation for handwriting skills. A child should be able to copy basic geometric shapes such as circles, plus signs, squares, and triangles before they are expected to write letters.

Ww

Make shadow puppets on the wall or floor.
A rabbit and spider, can you think of more?

28

Placing the hands into novel positions requires motor planning, the ability to figure out how to do an unfamiliar movement. Motor planning is needed for fine motor control and allows children to learn new tasks.

Xx

Sign the alphabet, a to x y z.
Start at the beginning, that is the key.

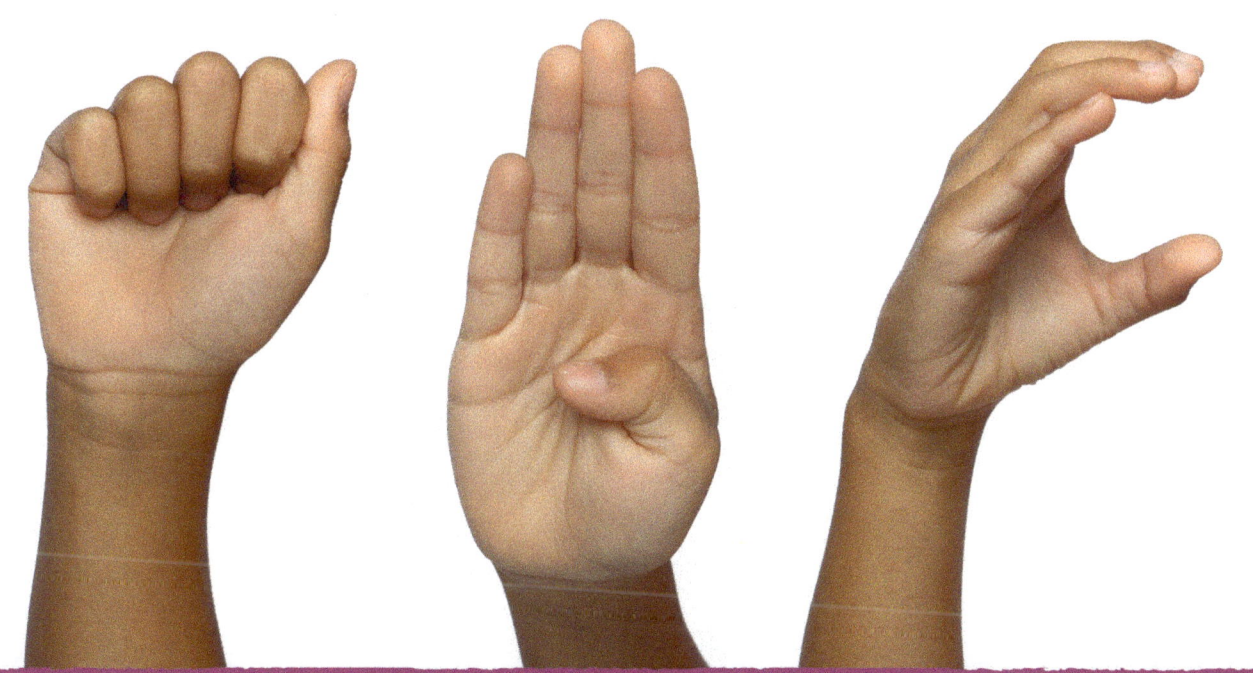

In addition to developing fine motor skills, sign language provides a kinesthetic, or physical, approach to learning the alphabet. The varied hand positions help to develop the arches of the hand, thumb opposition, hand separation, and finger isolation.

Yy

Pinch and rip to tear paper apart.
Glue down the pieces to create your own art.

Ensure that children are given the opportunity to use their creativity when doing fine motor projects. Giving them the freedom to create their own work instead of directly copying an example can increase interest and encourage participation.

Zz

Button, **zip**, tie, and snap.
Once you're done, give yourself a clap.

Practicing fine motor tasks within the context of a functional activity is the best way to develop skills and build independence. In addition to these fastener tasks, a child can work on functional hand skills by opening and closing containers such as jars, toothpaste tubes, and plastic zip bags.

Sensory ABC

Alphabet Themed Activities for Sensory Enrichment

Skill Builder Books

skillbuilderbooks.com

Stacie Erfle, MS, OTR/L

Aa

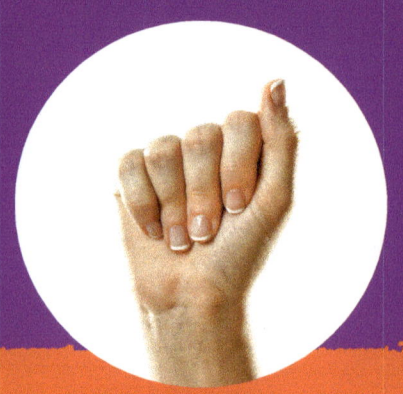

Help carry groceries and then put them away.
In the fridge, pantry, or cupboard and then go play.

34

Sensory rich activities do not always require special equipment or need to be complex. Even basic chores that involve lifting and carrying heavy items provide proprioceptive input. This type of sensation comes from the muscles and joints and provides the foundation for body awareness and body positioning.

Bb

Move your **body** all around, twirl and bend your knees. Dance to the music, but when it stops it's time to freeze.

Movement is sensed by the vestibular system, which is located in the inner ear and affects posture, balance, coordination, and attention. Spinning, swinging, and being upside down provide the most powerful and long-lasting input; however, all types of movement stimulate the vestibular system.

Cc

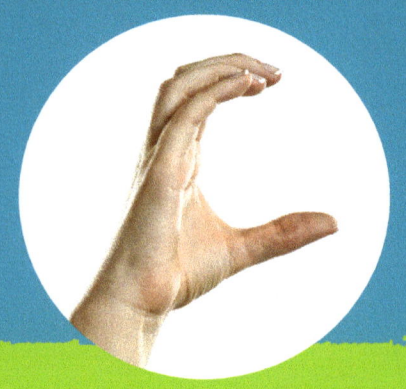

Inhale through your nose as arms reach overhead. Blow out your **candle** fingers, then it's off to bed.

Deep breathing is an invaluable tool for self-calming. This breathing exercise can be repeated 5 to 10 times and is even more beneficial when pushing the palms firmly against each other to elicit proprioceptive input. Including sensory activities into daily routines, such as bedtime, provides consistency and helps to prepare the body for what comes next.

Dd

Fidgets help your hands when they want to feel and move.
They shouldn't **distract,** for your attention they can improve.

Fidget toys can be purchased or simply made by putting materials such as rice or flour into an empty balloon or beads on a cord. They provide a way for children to get desired proprioceptive and tactile (touch) input discreetly while remaining seated and not disrupting others.

Ee

Can your hand tell what an object is without using your eyes? With only touch determine its texture, shape, and size.

38

The ability to identify something using only touch is called stereognosis. It requires accurate perception of the information that is being received from the hands. Movements are based on sensory feedback, therefore poor perception of touch input can lead to poor performance of fine motor skills.

Ff

Smear shaving cream on the mirror or even on the table. Use your finger to draw shapes or write words if you are able.

The tactile system is responsible for processing the information received from the skin. Exposure to a wide variety of tactile sensations, including messy play, helps children become accustomed to different textures. Food coloring can be added to the shaving cream for increased visual interest.

Gg

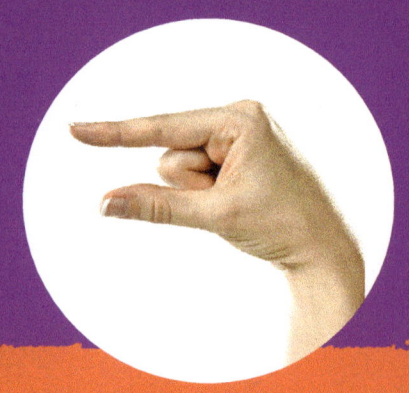

Wake your body up by pretending you're a log and roll.
Or choose a slow and gentle swing if calming is your **goal**.

Sensations can be calming or alerting to the body. In the case of vestibular input, movement that is linear, repetitive, and rhythmic helps to calm, while movement that is rotational, irregular, and fast helps to alert.

Hh

Get involved in preparing food, you can **help** make lunch.
Try it all, how does it taste, when you crunch and munch?

In addition to the sensory input received while cooking (touching, smelling, mashing, stirring, pouring, carrying, etc.), having children participate in preparation increases the likelihood they will try new foods. When planning meals, ensure that children are exposed to a variety of food textures and tastes, also known as gustatory perceptions.

Ii

Pull and push to transport **items** in a basket or a box.
Fill it up with heavy things like laundry, books, or rocks.

Referred to as heavy work, whole body actions that include pushing and pulling activate the proprioceptive system. This type of input can have an organizing effect on the body and is most beneficial when provided in regular intervals throughout the day.

Jj

Arm squeezes and bear hugs can be done day or night. Giving pressure to your body will make you feel **just** right.

Deep pressure is processed by the tactile system and can be calming because it activates the part of the nervous system that is responsible for turning off the stress response. Teaching a child this technique provides them with a strategy to use whenever they are feeling upset or anxious.

Kk

Move like a **kangaroo** when changing from one thing to another. Stop playing and hop to the table when called by your mother.

Transitions (changing from one thing to another) can be problematic, however the inclusion of movement provides sensory input that can help focus a child and prepare them for the next activity. Additionally, giving advanced warning, allowing for closure of the previous task, and providing a clear picture of what is coming next helps to facilitate smooth transitions.

Ll

Pile a mound of cushions, blankets, and pillows too.
Then leap into the crash pad, but be safe in all you do.

Having a designated area to jump and crash is beneficial for children who seek out proprioceptive and vestibular sensations. By providing consistent and structured ways for children to obtain sensory input, it is less likely they will find inappropriate ways to meet those needs (i.e. crashing into people, jumping off furniture, etc.).

Mm

After a bath get a **massage** with some lotion.
Not too fast or too hard, just a slow soothing motion.

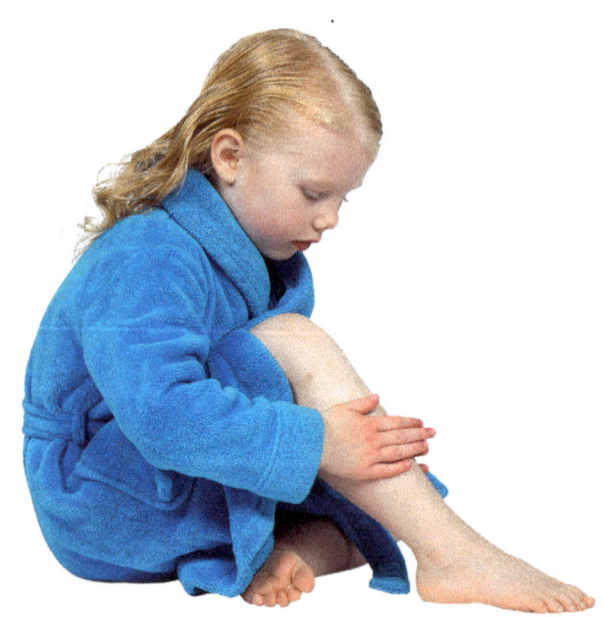

The tactile system is closely connected to the ability to be comforted and soothed, however it is dependent on the type of touch input. While deep pressure touch such as a massage can be relaxing and calming, light or unpredictable touch can be alerting.

Nn

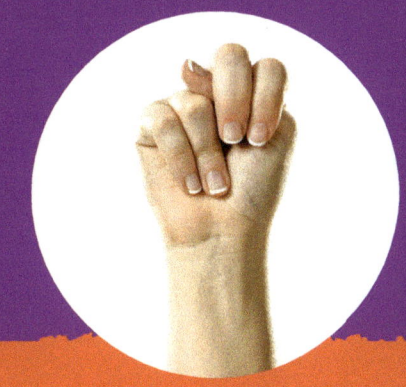

Scents can help you feel alert or calm from head to toes. It just depends what type of smells make it to your **nose.**

Strong smells such as citrus can be invigorating, while others such as lavender can be soothing. The sense of smell, or olfactory system, is tied closely to the part of the brain that is involved in memory and emotion and therefore can have a significant impact on behavior and mood.

If you're feeling **overwhelmed** with so many things in sight.
Take a break, remove distractions, and turn down the light.

Overstimulation can happen in any sensory system when a child is exposed to more sensory input than they are able to handle. In addition to low lighting, a clean and clutter free area reduces visual stimulation. This can be achieved by storing items in bins and covering book shelves with solid-colored fabric.

Pp

If the room seems small, **push** the wall with all your might. Did the space get any bigger? If not, that's alright.

Allowing young children opportunities for sensory input every 15 minutes can help with attention and participation. Movement reenergizes and refocuses the brain for learning. Performing this activity along with jumping jacks provides beneficial proprioceptive and vestibular input and is an effective "break" for both brains and bodies.

Qq

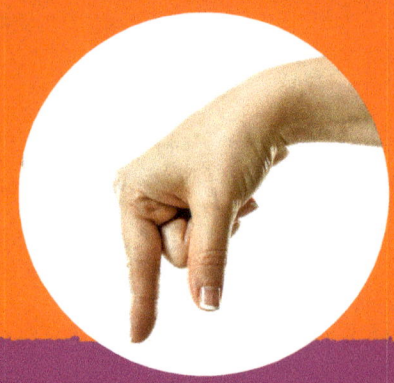

Focus on the noise, listen to the world with your ears. Try to guess the sounds, quiet whispers or loud cheers.

Hearing, referred to as the auditory system, includes the ability to process and interpret the sounds heard to give them meaning. When processing auditory information, the brain determines if a sound is important and requires immediate attention such as a fire alarm, or if it can be ignored such as the hum of a heater in the background.

Rr

Curl up like a ball with your forehead on the ground. With a calm, still body relax without a sound.

This position of full body flexion with deep pressure is intended to calm and can help minimize external stimulation. It can also be used after alerting activities to help a child return to a just right state (neither too energetic nor too lethargic).

Ss

Put birdseed, sand, beans, or rice into a big bin.
As you scoop, dig, and play how does it feel on your **skin?**

52

The tactile system has two parts, protective and discriminative. Protective touch includes pain and temperature and alerts to possible danger. Discriminative touch gives information about touch quality and characteristics such as texture, shape, and size.

Tt

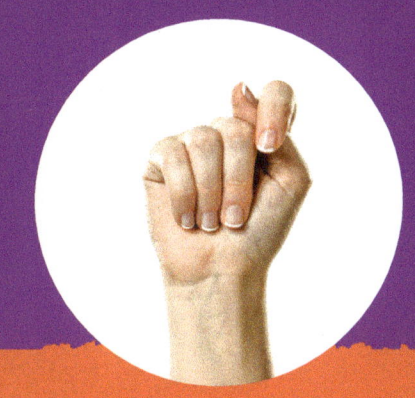

Use a **twisty** straw to drink a thick smoothie up.
What kind of fruit do you have in your cup?

Sucking against resistance, chewing, and eating crunchy food provides heavy work for the muscles of the mouth. This type of proprioceptive sensation, also called oral motor input, can have a calming and organizing effect on the body.

Uu

Build a course with obstacles to go over, **under**, and through. Use anything you have nearby, nothing needs to be new.

54

In addition to providing proprioceptive and vestibular input, obstacle courses create opportunities to work on activity sequencing, direction following, and praxis. Praxis includes coming up with an idea of how to move, planning the movement, and executing the action. It is required to carry out unfamiliar movements in a coordinated fashion.

Vv

Create a **very** special space designed just for you.
With things to help you unwind and feel at ease too.

When children are feeling overwhelmed or need a break, a sensory space provides a comforting retreat. It should include sensory tools that the individual child finds soothing such as a beanbag chair and soft music. In addition to being used to prevent a meltdown, these spaces aid in recovery after a child becomes upset.

Ww

When you need to get wiggles out but still stay in your seat.
Tie a stretchy band on chair legs and push it with your feet.

Sensory strategies should be used with the goal of increased success and participation in daily activities. Providing a way to get proprioceptive input while remaining seated in a chair allows a child to obtain organizing input that can improve their ability to attend to the teacher or focus on table top tasks.

Xx

Some feelings in your body can't be seen by an x-ray.
Like if you're feeling tired or need the bathroom right away.

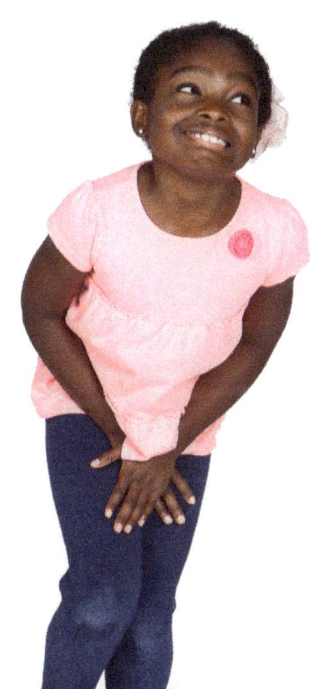

The perception of signals coming from inside the body (thirst, body temperature, etc.) is called interoception. Providing children frequent opportunities to check-in and listen to their body helps to build awareness and improves their ability to identify what they are feeling (I'm tired) and determine what action is needed (therefore I need to rest).

Yy

Go on a ride down the hall using a blanket or a sheet. Or you can do the pulling and let another have a seat.

Participation in sensory rich activities such as this allows for increased opportunities to experience varied input. The more "practice" a sensory system has processing information, the more effectively it can interpret sensations and respond to them appropriately.

Zz

With strong hands and arms lift your body off the chair. Count down from ten to **zero** keeping your feet in the air.

Chair push-ups can be held as described or done in repetition. Not only does this activity provide proprioceptive input to the arms, it engages the abdominals to address core stability. When done prior to fine motor tasks it prepares the trunk, arms, and hands for optimal skill performance.

Gross Motor ABC

Alphabet Themed Activities to Strengthen Gross Motor Skills

Skill Builder Books

skillbuilderbooks.com

Stacie Erfle, MS, OTR/L

Aa

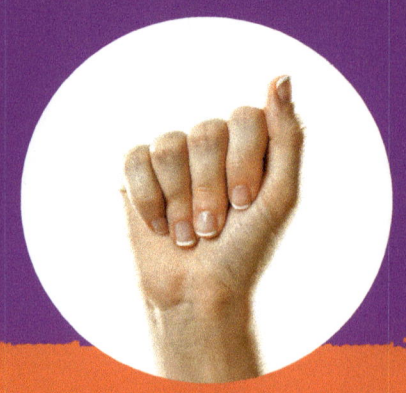

From hands and knees extend your right toes.
Then reach with left fingers, like an **arrow** you pose.

Gross motor skills involve the large muscles of the body - the arms, legs, and core, which includes of the muscles of the abdomen, pelvis, and back. They are developed through experience and repetition. This activity addresses balance, coordination, and strength, all of which are key gross motor components.

Bb

Row, row, row your **boat** to make your belly strong.
Take deep breaths, count to ten, or even sing a song.

Abdominal strength is an essential piece of core/trunk stability. A stable trunk creates a strong foundation that allows for coordinated movements of the arms and legs. Adequate core strength and stability is required for countless functional tasks, everything from sitting up at the table to eat to running and jumping on the playground.

Cc

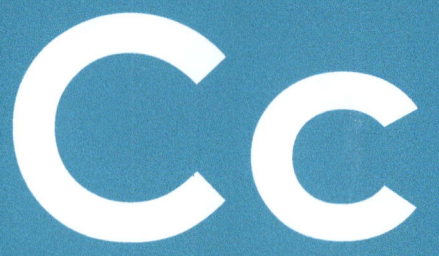

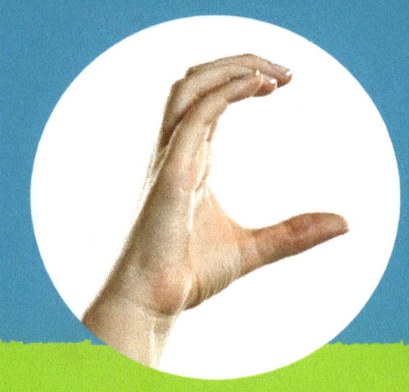

Get **creative** with your body and make the shape of a letter.
Move to spell words, the longer the better.

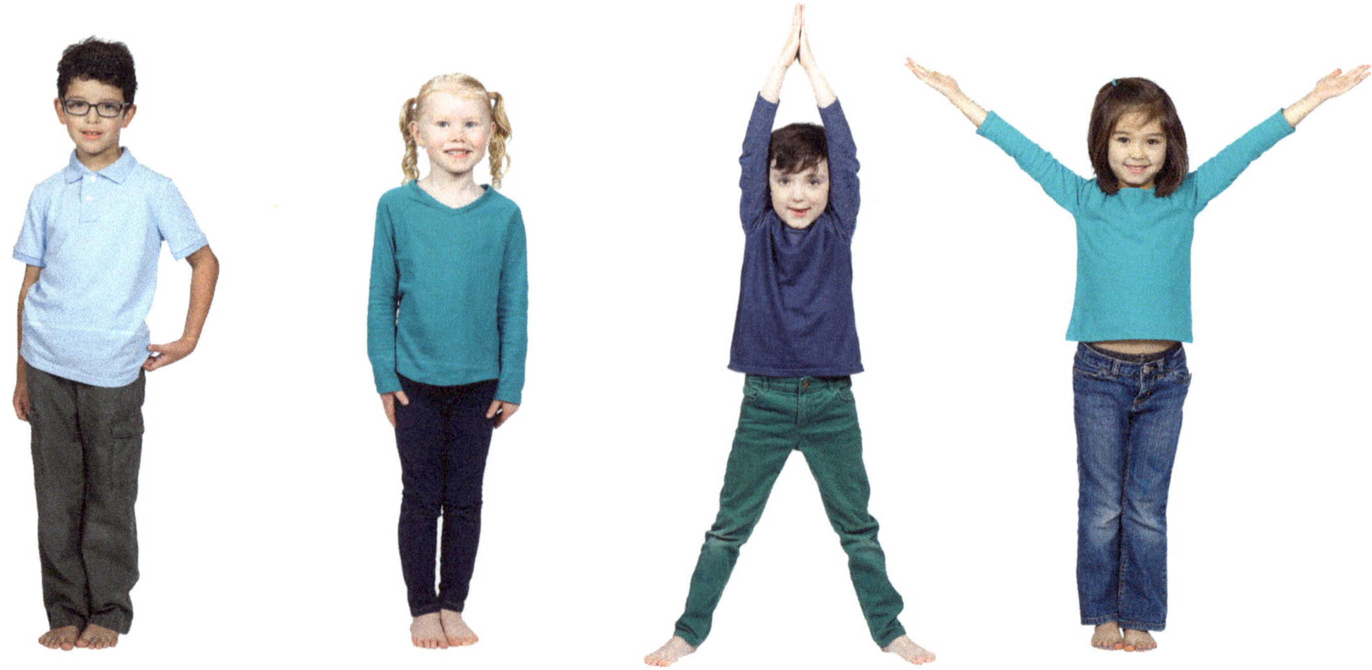

Combining movement with literacy activities provides an opportunity for kinesthetic learning. This occurs when a child learns concepts through physical activity instead of sitting and listening and/or looking at information. Learning can occur more readily when including the mind and the body.

Dd

Make an elephant trunk and reach it down to one shin. Lift it up on a **diagonal**, then back down again.

The midline divides the body into right and left sides. Movements that cross the midline promote communication between the two sides of the brain and require the two sides of the body to work together, known as bilateral coordination. The ability to spontaneously cross midline is vital to the development of hand dominance, reading, and writing.

Ee

Bend your **elbows** to make shelves for your knees.
Lift your toes off the ground and balance with ease.

This is a difficult pose that may require significant practice prior to mastery. Gross motor challenges build confidence, encourage persistence, and facilitate goal setting. Exposure to challenging tasks within a supportive environment can help a child view adversity as an opportunity for growth rather than an unsolvable problem.

Ff

Be strong like a warrior and flex your arms just so.
With your back leg straight, bend your front knee to sink low.

The focus of this task appears to be the arms and legs, however trunk stability is essential to obtain and maintain this position. Instead of allowing the lower back to sway, tuck the tailbone toward the ground and keep the hips facing forward to activate the core.

Gg

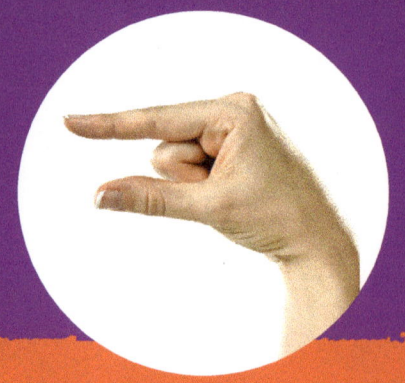

With one leg as the trunk and arms reaching high. Stand tall like a tree growing up to the sky.

Having an unmoving focal point promotes balance and helps to focus attention on the task. If a child is not yet able to balance on one leg successfully, this activity can be modified by keeping the toes of the bent leg on the ground or holding onto a wall or chair for added support.

Hh

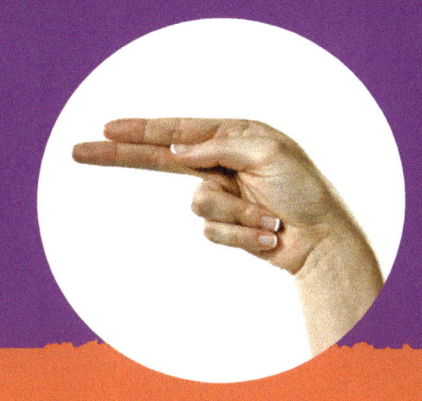

Bounce a small ball off the floor or the wall.
Catch it with one **hand** or two, you make the call.

Sensors in the muscles and joints provide feedback to the brain known as proprioceptive input. This is required for understanding body position, body awareness, and the amount of force required to carry out a task. For this activity, a child must grade their movements accurately, meaning the throw must be performed with neither too little nor too much force.

Ii

With forearms down **imagine** you're a dolphin in the ocean.
Shift your chin past your hands as an extra challenge motion.

Gross motor skills and fine motor skills are closely related. The trunk and shoulders must be stable before there can be precise control of the hands for activities such as writing and cutting. This movement activates the core as well as strengthens the shoulders through imaginative play, encouraging creativity along with supporting physical development.

Jj

Start crouched like a frog, hands and feet on the ground.
Then **jump** in the air and make a ribbit sound.

While gross motor activities are beneficial when performed individually, the inclusion of a group component facilitates social interactions. Simple group games such as tag, Simon Says, and Red Light Green Light can all be played using a variety of animal movements to encourage motor skill development along with cooperation and communication.

Kk

Bend your knees to sit, but a chair is not there.
Hold the position of your legs and lift your arms to the air.

Math concepts can easily be incorporated into gross motor activities. A child can count how long a body position is held or count the number of movement repetitions. Another simple way is to write various numbers on the ground with sidewalk chalk and have a child answer a math problem by jumping to the correct number.

Ll

Make a bridge with your body by **lifting** your hips.
Press down with your arms and put a smile on your lips.

Many gross motor movements provide the body with multiple benefits. In the case of bridge pose, it stretches the chest and hips while strengthening the back and legs. For proper positioning, press the arms into the floor, keep the legs parallel, the feet flat, and the chin lifted instead of tucked into the neck.

Mm

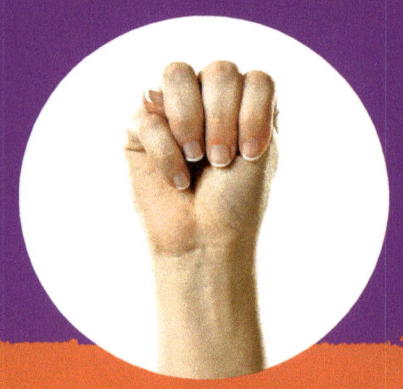

Touch opposite elbow to opposite knee.
Make them meet in the **middle**, move slow and carefully.

74

Performance of skilled movement is dependent on accurate perception of sensory input. This activity relies on input from the vestibular system. The vestibular system provides information about balance, the position of the head, and coordinates movements allowing both sides of the body to work together.

Nn

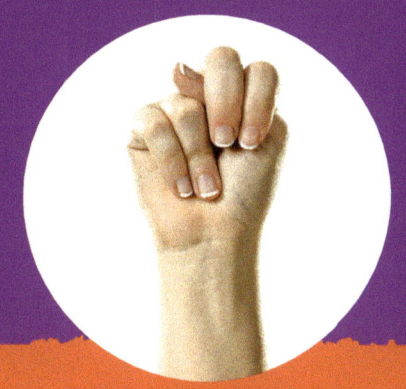

Lay on your back and pedal your legs fast or slow. Pretend you're riding a bike, **now** decide where to go.

Including imaginative play with gross motor activities is a creative way to make moving fun and engaging. A person who enjoys being physically active when young is more likely to continue with healthy activity patterns through adulthood.

Oo

Hips to the sky with fingers and toes on the land.
Lift one leg to balance, then add the **opposite** hand.

76

Pp

Walk down a **path** touching heel to toe.
Put tape on the floor so you know where to go.

This activity is a great way to work on balance without the use of a balance beam. In addition to forward heel to toe walking, a child can walk backwards, on tiptoes, sideways, or even with a bean bag balanced on their head. When completing the task, encourage the child to stay on the tape as if they were on an actual balance beam.

Qq

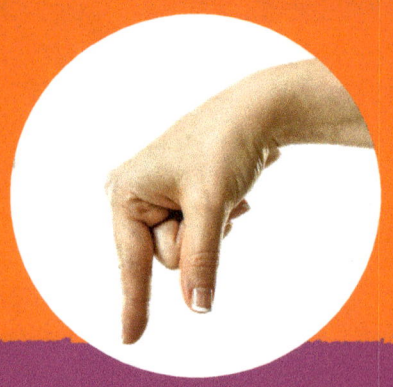

Creep your body forward like a leopard on the prowl.
Move one arm then the other and let out a quiet growl.

This movement is an example of reciprocal bilateral coordination, where the arms are moving in opposite (one forward and one back) and alternating (right arm then left arm) ways. Symmetrical bilateral coordination occurs when the two sides of the body mirror each other, such as clapping hands together.

Rr

Begin to skip with a step and a hop.
Left leg then **right** leg, alternate until you stop.

Prior to being able to skip, a child must be able to balance on one foot and hop. In addition to the movement of the legs, mature skipping includes forward motion of the arm opposite the lifted foot. Because skipping is a whole body coordination challenge, it is more difficult than other forms of locomotion, such as galloping.

Ss

Lay on your belly and lift your arms off the floor. Then add your legs, like a **superhero** you soar.

Core strengthening is not just about abdominal exercises. This movement strengthens the muscles of the back, which are equally important to trunk stability and upright posture. Holding the arms at the side instead of overhead is one way to change the activity to make it easier. Most gross motor activities can be adapted to meet a child's individual needs.

Tt

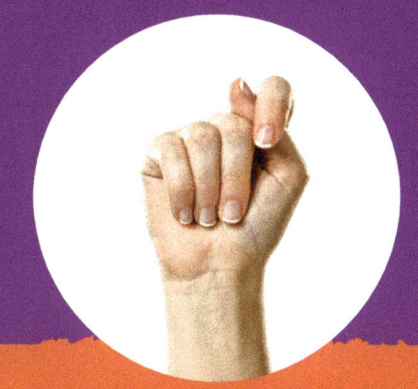

Start with a **target** close and move it away as you go.
With the ball in your hand, step with opposite foot and throw.

As with all skills, there is a developmental progression for throwing. First a child will throw overhand without including the lower body in the movement. Next they will step forward with the same foot as the throwing arm. Eventually they will progress to a mature throwing pattern, which includes stepping forward with the opposite foot.

Uu

Jump in all directions - forward, backward, left, and right. Keep your feet together and spring **up** to a great height.

Incorporating directional terms with movement reinforces the development of laterality (awareness of left and right sides of own body) and directionality. This allows a child to identify where objects are and where they are in relation to those objects. Directional awareness includes concepts of left/right, up/down, in/out, top/bottom, and front/back.

Vv

Keep your body **very** straight and like a lizard scurry. With small reptile steps, go slow or try to hurry.

While gross motor skills are often fun and games, they are vital to a child's development and independent functioning. Adequate gross motor skills are required for: locomotion, safely navigating environments, interacting with objects (holding, catching, throwing), active play (climbing, jumping, crawling), and self-care skills (dressing, eating, bathing).

Ww

Place your hands on the ground shoulder width apart. Walk your feet up the **wall** until they're above your heart.

Being upside down, also known as inverted, increases the blood flow to the brain and stimulates the vestibular system. The vestibular system is responsible for balance, coordination, and arousal level. This position strengthens the shoulders and arms and can be made more difficult by walking the feet higher up the wall.

Xx

Just like an X jump your arms and legs wide.
Then spring feet together and bring arms to your side.

Once a basic jumping jack has been mastered, varied arms movements can be added such as alternating arms overhead or clapping hands in front and behind the body. Incorporating new movement patterns will challenge a child's ability to plan and carry out non-habitual movements, also known as motor planning.

Yy

Reach for **your** toes, bend at your hips to fold.
Try to keep your back and legs straight, stretch and hold.

Stretching is beneficial to maintain flexibility and prevent injuries. When stretching after a physical activity, a child should stretch to the point of muscle tightness, never pain, and hold the stretch for 20 to 30 seconds without bouncing.

Zz

Zip and zoom, run so fast.
Keep your body moving, how long can you last?

Cardiovascular endurance is how well the heart and lungs can deliver oxygen to the body, while muscular endurance relates to how long a muscle is able to repeatedly exert force. Improvements in both types of endurance increases the amount of time a child can engage in an activity without getting tired.

Skill Builder Books

CPSIA information can be obtained
at www.ICGtesting.com
Printed in the USA
LVHW071926210419
615025LV00004B/13/P